CAT vs TRUMP

CAT vs TRUMP

IS YOUR CAT SMARTER THAN DONALD TRUMP?

HEADLINE

Cataloguing in Publication Data is available from the British Library

Hardback ISBN 978 1 4722 5 924 0

Designed by Beau Merchant at Toy Soldier Creative

Printed and bound in Great Britain by Clays Ltd, Elcograf S.p.A.

Headline's policy is to use papers that are natural, renewable and recyclable
products and made from wood grown in well-managed forests and other
controlled sources. The logging and manufacturing processes are expected
to conform to the environmental regulations of the country of origin.

HEADLINE PUBLISHING GROUP
An Hachette UK Company
Carmelite House
50 Victoria Embankment
London
EC4Y 0DZ

www.headline.co.uk
www.hachette.co.uk

'It is a difficult matter to gain the affection of a cat. He is a philosophical, methodical animal, tenacious of his own habits, fond of order and neatness, and disinclined to extravagant sentiment. He will be your friend, if he finds you worthy of friendship, but not your slave.'

Théophile Gautier

'I'm very highly educated. I know words – I have the best words.'

Donald J. Trump

INTRODUCTION

You remember Donald Trump, right? Wobbly orange trumpet on legs. Owner of a haircut more dodgy than every 80s popstar and 90s footballer combined. The answer to the question: 'What would the offspring of a Cheese Puff and a Dolphin look like?' He also happens to be the 45th President of the United States of America. To hold such an esteemed office surely requires an enormous amount of intelligence. Barack Obama went to Harvard, George W. Bush went to Yale, Donald Trump went to order more Chicken Nuggets but couldn't work the telephone. Despite seeming to possess less intelligence than a wok, Donald actually claims to be one of the smartest people on the planet:

'My IQ is one of the highest and you all know it! Please don't feel so stupid or insecure; it's not your fault.'

Quite a bold claim from a man who once also said:

'I don't get to watch much television, primarily because of documents. I am reading documents a lot and different things.'

It seems almost unfair to pit his intelligence against other humans. But what about if there was a way to compare how clever he is to your cat? On the face of it, this might seem like quite the insult (to your cat, of course), but, well, we all need an ego boost sometimes, don't we? This incredibly scientific test*, put together by some of the brightest minds in the world**, features physical and mental challenges for your cat, set alongside equivalent tests that Donald Trump has faced. Your job will be to observe your cat and try and guess how Donald fared, totting up the scores at the end to compare the two.

Now, some might accuse us of simply including a lot of tenuous examples of Trump being a moron in order to show him up as the absolute buffoon that he is, to which we respond—hey look over there! Is that a squirrel??

*well, sort of...
**See above

WHAT YOU WILL NEED

To complete the Cat vs Trump test you will need:

A cat

A pencil

The ability to forget that the world feels like it's on the brink of nuclear apocalypse for a bit

Instructions

Try to observe your cat without them being aware that you're watching them. It's vital not to influence their behaviour or collude with them to help them win (right, Donald?). Here is an example of the scoring system we'll be using, just to give you an idea:

How often has your cat colluded with Russia?	Score
Never	☐
A few times	☐
On several occasions	☐
All the damn time	☐

After careful observation you will need to make a record of your findings on the scorecard on page 79. Alongside each test for your cat you will see an equivalent challenge that Donny T was faced with. You should award him points depending on how you think he might have done – then turn to the scorecard to see how he actually did. Finally, compare scores to find out if your feline friend is indeed cleverer than The Donald, or whether you'll need to knit them a special little balaclava so they don't get bullied by all the other cats...

THE TEST

The test covers questions relating to four key behaviours common to both cats and The Orange One:

PROBLEM SOLVING

SOCIAL ACTIVITY

COORDINATION

COMMUNICATION SKILLS

SECTION 1:
PROBLEM SOLVING

'I love cats because I enjoy my home; and little by little, they become its visible soul.'

Jean Cocteau

'No more massive injections. Tiny children are not horses.'

Donald J. Trump

It may feel like Donald Trump has been president for several hundred years already, but his tenure has actually been fairly short. However, in that time the commander-in-chief has already come up against some hugely complex problems. Syria, for example, has been a big test. Having been briefed on the issue he was quick to fire back with some key questions: 'What is Syria?' 'When is it burger time?' 'Why is it called the Oval Office?'

Ultimately, at time of writing at least, he has failed to do anything about the Syria crisis other than poking that particular hornets' nest with his tiny orange fingers.

Cats, of course, have their own problems. ('Why hasn't the human fed me? It's been at least four minutes. And why are they trying to stop me eating grass again?') But who's better at coming up with solutions? Turn the page to find out!

1. Copycat test

Your cat observes you opening a cupboard door where its food is kept. Does it:

Remember what you've done and later manage to open the door and find its food ☐ 5 points

Attempt to open the door but without success ☐ 4 points

Stand by the door and mew ☐ 2 points

Ignore the door entirely ☐ 1 point

SECTION 1: PROBLEM SOLVING

Donald Trump was called on to give the commencement speech at Liberty University on May 13th, 2017, Did he:

Speak eloquently and inspirationally	☐	5 points
Share words of warmth and wisdom	☐	4 points
Read a solid if unspectacular speech	☐	2 points
Appear to plagiarise lines from the film *Legally Blonde*	☐	0 points

2. Patience Test

A stray box has been inadvertently placed in front of the catflap. Does your cat deal with the situation by:

Managing to move the box	☐	5 points
Finding you and mewing until you move the box	☐	4 points
Standing by the box, whining loudly and repeatedly until it is removed	☐	2 points
Giving up entirely	☐	1 point

SECTION 1: PROBLEM SOLVING

Trump's signature haircut (part puffin wing, part orange zest) has been under scrutiny for a while. Reportedly, Trump has turned to using hair dye. Does he solve the problem of fading colour by:

Applying the hair dye as per the instructions

☐   5 points

Ignoring the instructions but waiting for an appropriate amount of time when using the dye

☐   3 points

(According to Ivanka Trump) Removing the hair dye way earlier than instructed, resulting in the bizarre orangey-blonde colour

☐   0 points

3. Logic Test

Show your cat your upturned hands, a cat snack in one of them. Close your hands into fists and swap them back and forth a few times. Hold your still closed hands towards your cat. Does it:

Easily follow the right hand and watch it until you reveal the treat

☐ 5 points

Bat at both of your hands until you give it the treat

☐ 4 points

Give up and walk away

☐ 2 points

Stare vacantly at you

☐ 1 point

New York's second coldest New Year's Eve on record was recorded in Times Square in 2017. Did Donny von Trumpington:

Express concern that climate change is affecting the world

5 points

Advise citizens to keep warm

4 points

Say nothing

2 points

Tweet the following:
'In the East, it could be the COLDEST New Year's Eve on record. Perhaps we could use a little bit of that good old Global Warming that our Country, but not other countries, was going to pay TRILLIONS OF DOLLARS to protect against.'

0 points

4. What's the difference?

Place a packet of unopened cat food next to your cat's usual food bowl. Does it:

Look between the packet and the bowl, understanding what needs to happen next ☐ 5 points

Try to tear the packet open ☐ 4 points

Sniff the packet and walk away ☐ 2 points

During a fundraising speech in Florida in March 2018, Trump referred to an apparently gamechanging phonecall regarding the North Korean nuclear crisis, saying: 'They, by the way, called up a couple of days ago. They said, "we would like to talk. And I said, "so would we, but you have to denuke".' Was he:

Referencing a groundbreaking conversation with the North Korean Government

☐ 5 points

Apparently mistaking North Korea for South Korea, having actually been speaking to South Korea President Moon Jae-in

☐ 0 points

5. Clean Eating

After eating, you observe that your cat has a rather large amount of food trapped in its whiskers. Does it:

Quickly lick its paw and wipe the food away

5 points

Rub its face on a surface to try and remove the food

4 points

Ignore it entirely until you have to deal with it

2 points

In May 2016, Trump was under fire for deriding Mexicans. In order to build bridges, did the Buffoon-in-Chief:

Apologise and backtrack from his offensive comments

☐ 5 points

Tweet a picture of a taco bowl with the caption: 'Happy #CincoDeMayo! The best taco bowls are made in Trump Tower Grill. I love Hispanics!'

☐ 0 points

6. Border Patrol

Set up a short border in a doorway with a piece of cardboard. Does your cat:

Nimbly hop over the cardboard ☐ 5 points

Push it out the way ☐ 3 points

Mew until you move it ☐ 2 points

Having frequently touted the building of a border wall between the US and Mexico, did Trump calm fears over the practicalities of such an enterprise by:

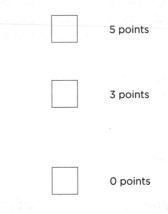

Immediately backtracking as soon as he was elected	☐	5 points
Considering more sensible alternatives	☐	3 points
Promising that he would build the wall but that it would have: 'a big beautiful door in it'.	☐	0 points

7. *Playing Teacher*

Believe it or not, but there are lots of excellent apps/ games that you can download on your phone to test your cat's mental agility (try 'Game for Cats' for iPhone or 'Crazy Cat' for Android — both are free). Demonstrate how to play the game to your cat at first. Does your cat respond by:

Joining in after its very first 'lesson' ☐ 5 points

Joining in, but after several 'lessons' ☐ 4 points

Watching you play but not responding itself ☐ 2 points

Getting bored and walking away ☐ 1 point

SECTION 1: PROBLEM SOLVING

Clearly deciding that he had too much wisdom to keep all to himself, in 2005 The Donald set up his very own university (imaginatively called 'Trump University'). But how did things pan out? Did Trump:

Foster a new generation of successful entrepreneurs, with the university going from strength to strength

5 points

Face some criticism but ultimately make the university a success

3 points

Close the University just five years after it opened, facing multiple lawsuits from angry 'students', eventually having to settle out of court in November 2016 to the tune of $35m

0 points

SECTION 2:
SOCIAL SKILLS

'My relationship with my cats has saved me from a deadly, pervasive ignorance.'

William S. Burroughs

'Do you mind if I sit back a little bit? Because your breath is very bad.'

Donald J. Trump

'Do I have social skills?' Donald Trump once asked a young crowd of people who were at the White House for a 'sport and fitness' day, according to the *New York Post*. 'I don't know,' Trump continued, answering his own question, 'but I have social media, that's for sure!' Classic Donald social skills, right there: ask a question, answer it yourself with a non-sequitur. It's very rare for Trump to have actual conversations with people, of course. If someone starts to talk when he doesn't want them to he has that particularly annoying habit of saying 'excuse me, excuse me!', his mouth puckered into a sparrow's cloaca, apparently affronted at the idea of anyone DARING to question him.

Cats' social skills tell us a lot about their intelligence: how do they deal with strangers? Are you able to train them to grow out of their unsociable habits?

We've gathered some scenarios here which involve monitoring your moggy's social behaviour, as well as some challenges which Donny T faced in his relentless pursuit of perfection (ahem!).

But who will come out on top? Turn the page to get cracking!

1. Stranger Things

A friend comes around that your cat hasn't met before. Does it:

Confidently approach to say hello	☐	4 points
Warily approach	☐	3 points
Run to its safe place	☐	1 point

SECTION 2: SOCIAL SKILLS

At a meeting of NATO leaders in May 2017, Trump found himself at the back of a group of people he didn't know. Did he:

Patiently wait his turn before engaging someone in the group in conversation at an appropriate time

  4 points

Quietly make his way off stage

  3 points

Barge the president of Montenegro out of the way so that he could stand at the front in view of the cameras

  0 points

2. Bye-bye!

A guest comes around and plays with your cat. After a while, your cat decides it would rather be alone. Does it:

Slink away but only after a final affectionate gesture like rubbing it's head on your guest's leg ☐ 4 points

Whine until your guest lets them go ☐ 3 points

Lash out at your guest ☐ 1 point

On 13 March, 2018, Donald Trump — as part of sweeping changes — fired Rex Tillerson, his Secretary of State. Did Trump break the news to Tillerson:

In a personal, face-to-face meeting ☐ 4 points

In a personally written letter ☐ 3 points

By tweeting the news shortly after Tillerson had been told by Trump's chief of staff while he was sitting on the toilet ☐ 0 points

3. Rulebreaker?

**You probably impose some sort of rules on your cat.
No sofa scratching, for example. Does your cat:**

Always abide by the rule   ☐   4 points

Attempt the odd cheeky
rule break   ☐   3 points

Consistently ignore you   ☐   1 point

In early March 2018 it was reported that Donald Trump had allegedly engaged in an extra-marital affair with a porn star called Stormy Daniels. Had the Trump team dealt with the issue by:

Coming clean about what actually happened

 4 points

Reportedly paying Daniels $130,000 hush money in 2016, something that some have argued constitutes breaking the rules of campaign financing

0 points

4. Sleep Well?

You wake to find your cat curled up and snoozing on your legs. If you try to extract them does it:

Rearrange itself without complaint	☐	4 points
Give a frustrated mew before moving	☐	3 points
Mew repeatedly until you return to the same position	☐	1 point

As Commander-in-Chief, you'd have thought Trump would need to be well rested to take on his job. So do Trump's sleeping habits include:

Getting a solid seven hours

4 points

Sleeping, according to the man himself, 'three hours, four hours' a night, at most, perhaps fuelled by his reportedly drinking up to 12 Diet Cokes a day

0 points

5. Sleep Well? (pt2)

Just like us, cats have dreams. They can often be complex as the cat relives lengthy sequences of events — signs that they are active and social. When dreaming, your cat's face and whiskers will often twitch. Observe your cat sleeping five times. How often does it appear to be dreaming?

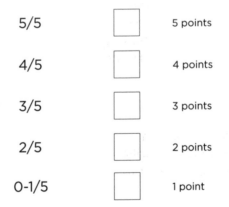

5/5	☐	5 points
4/5	☐	4 points
3/5	☐	3 points
2/5	☐	2 points
0-1/5	☐	1 point

SECTION 2: SOCIAL SKILLS

According to Barack Obama's personal aide, the 44th POTUS would wake up at 6am in order to work out for 45 minutes, before catching up with his family. But how about Donald-the-Trump? Does the big guy:

Follow a similar routine, in order to maximise his time spent on important issues and remain alert and sociable

4 points

Awake early to watch *Fox and Friends*, angrily live-tweeting it at stupid o'clock

0 points

6. You're so vain...

Your cat is strolling along minding its own business when it happens to catch its reflection in a mirror / the telly / a window. Does it:

Stop briefly to check its appearence before sauntering off ☐ 5 points

Walk past with barely a glance ☐ 3 points

Freak out completely ☐ 1 point

The leader of the free world is surely too busy to spend their mornings doing anything other than thinking about the challenges that lie ahead. When Donald John (you forget that he's got a relatively normal middle name sometimes) Trump rises, does he:

Spring into action, preparing for a day of important meetings and wondering how he can help people less fortunate than himself

 3 points

According to reports, receive and spend time going through a 'positive dossier' featuring screenshots of nice tweets about him and pictures from public appearances where he looks 'tough'

0 points

SECTION 3:
COMMUNICATION SKILLS

'A cat has absolute emotional honesty: human beings, for one reason or another, may hide their feelings, but a cat does not.'

Ernest Hemingway

'We see it in the mothers and the fathers . . . they sacrifice every day for the furniture and future of their children.'

Donald J. Trump

Donald Trump and 'communication skills' - two things that go together about as well as jam covered testicles and a thousand ants, or Piers Morgan and the concept of humility. We've collated some examples of Captain Trumpington's famously nuanced approach to social interaction and asked you to guess how well you think he did.

When it comes to cats, communication skills are another indicator of their intelligence. Does your kitty seek you out when it wants some affection? Does it make specific sounds when it needs something? Turn the page for another round of Cat vs Trump!

1. Resolving conflict

Not all of us can be perfect, which means you have the odd person (and we mean odd) who isn't that keen on cats. But if your moggy is a clever one they may be able to solve that problem. Confronted with an awkward stranger, does your cat:

Seeing that they are uncomfortable, come over and purr, showing your guest lots of affection
☐ 4 points

Ignore them entirely
☐ 3 points

Hiss and generally behave aggressively
☐ 1 point

Following a Presidential debate moderated by journalist Megyn Kelly, did Trump respond to her thorough line of questioning by:

Praising her skills as a combative interlocutor ☐ 4 points

Claiming that 'There was blood coming out of [Kelly's] eyes, there was blood coming out of her wherever.' ☐ 0 points

2. Unwelcome guests

A stranger knocks on the door (interrupting your valuable eating-cheese-in-your-pants time, no doubt). But does your cat respond by:

Immediately coming to say hello to their new friend and rubbing up against their legs

4 points

Slinking away to hide

2 points

Whining

1 point

In April 2018 the FBI raided the offices of Trump's personal lawyer, Michael Cohen. Did Trump communicate his response by:

Issuing a formal statement welcoming the investigation as important and necessary

4 points

Stay silent, waiting for due process to run its course

3 points

Begin an unrelated press conference by declaring: 'It's a disgraceful situation. It's a total witch hunt. I've been saying it for a long time.'

0 points

3. Speaking clearly

We all know our cats like telling us how they're feeling, no matter what we might be up to, but the sounds your cat makes offer clues to its intelligence. So, when it comes to vocal expressions, does your cat:

Have more than three clearly defined noises to help effectively communicate to you what it's after

☐ 4 points

Have one or two variations

☐ 3 points

Only make the same noise, no matter what it seems to be trying to tell you

☐ 1 point

On 6th December 2017, in a trademark piece of diplomacy, Trump decided to ignore all sensible advice and declared that the US would be recognising Jerusalem as the capital of Israel. When giving the speech, did Trump communicate his message:

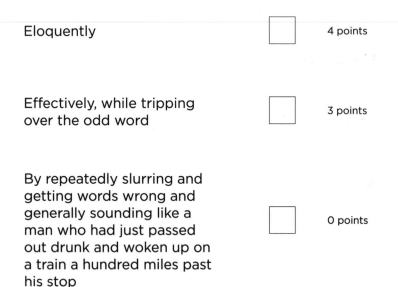

Eloquently   4 points

Effectively, while tripping over the odd word   3 points

By repeatedly slurring and getting words wrong and generally sounding like a man who had just passed out drunk and woken up on a train a hundred miles past his stop   0 points

4. Getting Attention...

How often does your cat 'trill' or 'chirrup' when it wants something from you?

Frequently ☐ 4 points

Sometimes ☐ 3 points

Never ☐ 1 point

As we all know, Donald spends a ridiculous amount of time seeking attention on Twitter. When questioned about this by puce-faced talking ham, Piers Morgan, did Trump respond by:

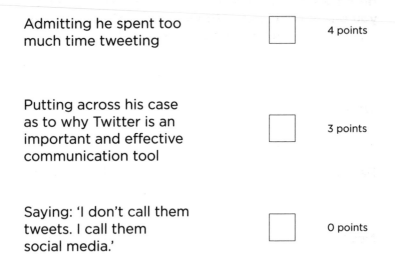

Admitting he spent too much time tweeting — 4 points

Putting across his case as to why Twitter is an important and effective communication tool — 3 points

Saying: 'I don't call them tweets. I call them social media.' — 0 points

5. Show Some Affection

We all need a pat on the back every now and then (or a tummy rub, for that matter), and our cats are no different. But is your cat smart enough to seek you out when it wants to feel the love? Note down whether this happens:

Often ☐ 4 points

Rarely ☐ 3 points

Never ☐ 1 point

The 2011 Correspondents' dinner seems a million years ago now, right? Watching clips of Obama almost affectionately teasing Trump for his part in the birther conspiracy seems like it happened in a simpler time. You may know the answer to this one already, but can you remember if Trump responded by:

Taking the jokes in good
spirit and laughing along

4 points

Smiling but looking a little
awkward

3 points

Sitting stoney-faced, miserably,
ultimately so thin-skinned that
it caused him to embark on a
vendetta against Obama that
led him to the presidency and
the massive crap-storm we
currently find ourselves in

0 points

6. Trust

When cats trust us they communicate this by blinking slowly, as having their eyes closed is when they are at their most vulnerable. They are showing us they know we aren't a threat. But how often does your cat do this?

Often   ☐   4 points

Occassionally   ☐   3 points

Never   ☐   1 point

The USA has perhaps the finest intelligence community in the world. When they told Trump that Russia had meddled in the US election, did he:

Trust them completely ☐ 4 points

Say that he trusted them but with some reservations ☐ 3 points

Initially at least refuse to trust them, saying: '[Putin] said he didn't meddle, he said he didn't meddle. I asked him again. You can only ask so many times' ☐ 0 points

7. Loyalty

OK, so we're not as naive as to think that our cats daydream about us when we're not there, but you'd like to think they still feel some loyalty to us, not just whoever's carrying the biggest treat. The next time you're away for a while, observe whether your cat makes a point of saying hello when you return. Does this happen:

Often ☐ 4 points

Occasionally ☐ 3 points

Never ☐ 0 points

Fired FBI director and guy who definitely-didn't-mess-up-the-whole-election-with-that-last-minute-emails-thing Jim Comey revealed that Trump requested what from him at a weirdly intimate dinner:

Honesty | 4 points

Fairness | 3 points

Loyalty | 0 points

SECTION 4: COORDINATION SKILLS

'The smallest feline is a masterpiece.'

Leonardo da Vinci

'I was gonna hit one guy in particular, a very little guy. I was gonna hit this guy so hard his head would spin and he wouldn't know what the hell happened... I was going to hit a number of those speakers so hard their heads would spin, they'd never recover. And that's what I did with a lot – that's why I still don't have certain people endorsing me: they still haven't recovered.'

Donald Trump

If we were being immature, we'd use some of this section to make jokes about Trump and his campaign allegedly coordinating with the Russians before and during the election, or Trump allegedly coordinating with his lawyers to arrange hush money payments...

For cats, physical coordination is a very important part of their lives. We've all looked on enviously as a cat glances lazily up at a high wall and elegantly leaps up there. Here are a few tests for you to carry out to see just how coordinated your cat is, to be judged very scientifically against Trump's best coordination efforts...

1. Ball Games

Gently roll a tennis ball towards your cat. Does it:

Bat it back towards you ☐ 5 points

Attack it ☐ 3 points

Ignore it entirely ☐ 1 point

The orange Shrek tweeted 27 times disparagingly about his predecessor playing golf. So how many times has he hit the course since taking office?

A few times 4 points

Several times [ ] 1 point

At the time of writing, 116 times since becoming president [ ] 0 points

2. That's Handy

Place your hand just above your cat's head and say the words 'high five'. If it touches your hand with its paw, give it a treat. Repeat several times. Does your cat:

Immediately pick up the trick and continue to high-five you even without a treat

5 points

Learn the trick initially but then forget it later on

3 points

Not pick up the trick at all

1 point

You've just been made president of the most powerful country in the world. You greet a series of leaders from around the globe. Do you:

Offer and execute a traditional handshake 4 points

Do something a bit awkward like go in for a hug by mistake 3 points

Perform a series of bizarre, push-me-pull-you movements, grimacing and gripping on as hard as you can, in no way compensating for a TINY . . . amount of intelligence 0 points

3. When The Bubble Bursts

Using a bubble blower and (cat-friendly) solution, blow some bubbles in the air where your cat is. Does it:

Jump up and bat the
bubbles midair

5 points

Wait until they land before
trying to pounce

3 points

Ignore them entirely

1 point

As of June 2018, the Russia investigation is still very much up in the air, bubbling away (what do you mean, 'that's a tenuous link'?). Faced with the ongoing scandal, has Trump:

Kept quiet and allowed the investigators to carry on unimpeded

4 points

Occassionally raised concerns about the process

1 points

Continually claimed the investigation is a 'WITCH HUNT' and threatened to pardon himself if convicted of any wrongdoing

0 points

4. Bit Of A Leap

Observe the times when your cat jumps from one object onto another. Does it:

Consistently land cleanly ☐ 5 points

Have the occasional wobble ☐ 3 points

Frequently miss its
intended landing place ☐ 1 point

SECTION 4: COORDINATION SKILLS

One of the trickiest things as a world leader is to seem in control at all times on the grandest of stages. When Trump was faced with drinking from a bottle of water during a speech did he:

Complete the task like an ordinary human being

 4 points

Slightly spill some of the water

☐ 1 point

Drink from the bottle with two hands, tipping it up-wards into his face, as if he'd never seen a bottle of water in his life before, despite having previously mocked a senator for the way he drank water

☐ 0 points

5. A Tough Exercise

Another favourite pastime for our cats is climbing trees. How they fare in their adventuring can be a clear indicator of intelligence. So how does your cat get on when climbing trees? Does it:

Scamper merrily up and down with no issues

☐   5 points

Get up there OK but have the occasional tricky moment climbing back down

☐   3 points

Fail to get up, or get up but then fail to get back down

☐   1 point

In February 2018, Trump was recorded talking to members of Congress about his recent physical exam. Did he:

Reveal that he learned lots about his physicality and vowed to improve his fitness

 4 points

Claimed the test had been tough but that he'd passed without many issues

 1 point

Boast at being able to run for nine minutes on a treadmill, claiming that he said to the doctor: 'What do I have to prove? I'm telling you, I could have gone much longer.'

 0 points

6. Boxing Clever

Put a soft toy on a string and show it to your cat. Next, take a cardboard box and show your cat that you've hidden the toy under the box with the string still showing. Does your cat:

Work out how to get under the box to find the toy ☐ 5 points

Wait for you to lift the box before pouncing ☐ 3 points

Show no interest in the game ☐ 1 point

When interviewed for one of his many genius works of literature, Trumpington was asked about whether he was sporty in his youth. Did he respond by:

Explaining in a self-deprecating way that, no, have you seen me, of course I wasn't.

 4 points

Modestly explaining some sporting success he'd had along the way

 3 points

Saying: 'I was always the best athlete . . . I was always the best at sports.'

 0 points

7. Having A Ball

Ideally on a firm-ish floor, sit opposite your cat and bounce a ping-pong ball towards it. Does your cat:

Instantly bat the ball back, continuing to do so as long as you play

☐ 5 points

Try but fail to hit the ball

☐ 3 points

Show no interest in the game

☐ 1 point

In 2016, the *Washington Post* reported that Trump believed what about fitness?

That the more you exercise and learn the more you improve coordination

4 points

That, while it wasn't his favourite thing to do, he was clever enough to realise keeping fit was important

3 points

That the human body was 'like a battery, with a finite amount of energy, which exercise only depleted'

0 points

8. Is That Cheating?

**Head back to your online application store. There are specific games there to help with your cat's coordination ('Laser Chase' for example).
Does your cat:**

Show great interest and
aptitude for the games — 5 points

Paw wildly at the screen
whether there's a game
loaded or not — 3 points

Show no interest
whatsoever — 1 point

Those moments where leaders have to appear in front of the press with their partners can be awkward to coordinate and choreograph, but it just takes a bit of intelligence to get through them without issue. So... on March 2nd, 2018, when Trump and his wife Melania were faced with 40mph winds on the runway, did Trump:

Wait for his wife to arrive at his side before walking hand in hand up onto Airforce One

4 points

Wait for her to arrive at his side but go up the stairs first

3 points

Completely ditch her without a backwards glance

0 points

RESULTS!

Congratulations on completing the intensive - and very scientific - Cat vs Trump test! Hopefully you will have recorded your cat's efforts on the scorecard on page 79. It's time to tot them up and answer the ultimate question - is your cat smarter than Donald J. Trump?!

Well, well, well - what a surprise, your cat is more intelligent than the President of the United States of America! Who'da thunk it, eh? Here is some closer analysis on your cat depending on their score for each section:

SECTION 1:

SCORE RANGE: 0-8 Little bit smarter than Trump

SCORE RANGE: 9-19 Definitely smarter than Trump

SCORE RANGE: 20-28 Streets ahead of the tangerine clown

SCORE RANGE: 29-35 Basically Robert Mueller

SECTION 2:

SCORE RANGE: 0-5 Little bit smarter than Trump

SCORE RANGE: 6-12 Definitely smarter than Trump

SCORE RANGE: 13-20 Streets ahead of the tangerine clown

SCORE RANGE: 21-26 Basically Robert Mueller

SECTION 3:

SCORE RANGE: 0-6 Little bit smarter than Trump

SCORE RANGE: 9-13 Definitely smarter than Trump

SCORE RANGE: 14-20 Streets ahead of the tangerine clown

SCORE RANGE: 21-28 Basically Robert Mueller

SECTION 4:

SCORE RANGE: 0-10 Little bit smarter than Trump

SCORE RANGE: 11-20 Definitely smarter than Trump

SCORE RANGE: 21-30 Streets ahead of the tangerine clown

SCORE RANGE: 31-40 Basically Robert Mueller

TOTAL SCORE RANGES

0-29
Smarter than Trump

30-64
Smarter than Trump AND Mike Pence
put together

65-98
Bona Fide Genius Cat

99-129
Run for Office 2020!

CAT	TRUMP
SECTION 1:	**SECTION 1:**
1.... 2.... 3.... 4....	1Ò.. 2O.. 3Ò.. 4O..
5.... 6.... 7....	5Ò.. 6O.. 7O..
SCORE......	SCORE O..
SECTION 2:	**SECTION 2:**
1.... 2.... 3.... 4....	1O.. 2Ò.. 3Ò.. 4O..
5.... 6....	5O.. 6O..
SCORE......	SCORE......
SECTION 3:	**SECTION 3:**
1.... 2.... 3.... 4....	1Ò.. 2O.. 3Ò.. 4O..
5.... 6.... 7....	5Ò.. 6O.. 7O..
SCORE......	SCORE O..
SECTION 4:	**SECTION 4:**
1.... 2.... 3.... 4....	1Ò.. 2O.. 3O.. 4O..
5.... 6.... 7.... 8....	5O.. 6Ò.. 7O.. 8O..
SCORE......	SCORE O..

NOTES

NOTES

NOTES

NOTES

NOTES

NOTES

NOTES

NOTES

NOTES

NOTES

NOTES